The Knitter's Companion
101 Handy Hints

Anne Willis

Kangaroo Press

To my mother, who taught me to knit at a very early age; to Susanne, who encouraged me to go beyond the basics, and to my husband, who helped to edit the manuscript and has put up with clicking needles for the last twenty-nine years.

Acknowledgments

The techniques in this book are a distillation of countless different patterns over the years, of tips from friends, my own inventions, of ideas from many knitting publications. Sources which I have found particularly useful include:

Een Recht, Een Averecht by Nora Hana, The Hague

Golden Hands

Vogue Knitting

Elizabeth Zimmermann's Knitting Workshop

I would like to thank Colin Medlycott, Manhattan Photographics and Kim Cottrell for illustrating this book. Cover photograph courtesy Robyn Malcolm.

First published in 1993 by Kangaroo Press Pty Ltd
3 Whitehall Road Kenthurst NSW 2156
P.O. Box 6125 Dural Delivery Centre NSW 2158 Australia
Typeset by G.T. Setters Pty Limited
Printed in Hong Kong through Colorcraft Ltd

ISBN 0 86417 526 4

Contents

1 Casting on

Before casting on *always* make a tension square! This might seem very boring, but it is the basis for the success of your work. You will see it stressed in every knitting pattern, and it really is very important. When you use a different yarn from the one prescribed by the pattern, remember to measure not only the width (stitches), but also the length (rows) per 10 cm.

There are many different ways of casting on and no doubt everybody has a favourite way of doing it. I have tried many and have come to the conclusion that the two ways below are both very strong. The second way is invisible in knit 1, purl 1 bands (see **Photo 1**), and both keep the bands from stretching.

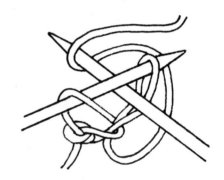

Diagram 1: Cast on knitwise

1. Casting on with 2 needles

I use this for all casting on except knit 1, purl 1 rib. Make a loop and put it on a needle. Put the point of the second needle through the loop and make 1 stitch knitwise, but instead of sliding it off the left-hand needle, put the made loop on the left-hand needle. Now put the right-hand needle point through the space between the first and second stitches (see Diagram 1) and make a new stitch as before. This will be easier if you pull the stitch tight after you have inserted the needle. Continue until the right number of stitches has been made (see **Photo 2**).

2. Casting on with 2 needles in knit 1, purl 1 rib

Start as for the previous method. When you have 2 loops on the left-hand needle, make the next stitch purlwise, i.e. put the point of the right-hand needle between the two previous stitches *from the back* (see Diagram 2) and make the stitch as before. The next stitch is made knitwise. Alternate making stitches purlwise and knitwise. Check regularly, because if you make a mistake the ribbing on the next row will not fit. It helps if you count aloud as

Diagram 2: Cast on purl stitch through back

you make your stitches: you must be making a knit stitch when you count an even number. On the next row knit 1, purl 1, but work the knit stitches in the back of the loop on the first row only.

Sewing up the rib

Disregard the number of stitches prescribed by your knitting pattern for casting on for knit 1, purl 1 rib (called 1 X 1 rib) if it gives an uneven number. *Always* use an even number of stitches for 1 X 1 rib because, when you sew up your work, the first and the last stitch disappear to the back. With an even number of stitches you are still left with a knit and a purl stitch after sewing up, so the rib appears continuous. With an uneven number you have a knit stitch at each end so that when you sew up the work you have two purl stitches left, one from the front and one from the back, next to one another, which makes a wide gap.

If your pattern for the first row of the rib reads: 'K2, p1, k1, and end with k2', one of the knit stitches of the front and of the back will fall away to the inside, leaving you with 2 knit stitches. In this case also the sewn-up rib will not be continuous.

For a knit 2, purl 2 rib (called 2 X 2 rib), you must have a number of stitches divisible *not* by 4, but by 2, so you should always start with knit 2 and end with knit 2; one of the 2 knit stitches

falls away to the inside when sewing the seam, which leaves you with one knit stitch from the front and one from the back, making two again, so that the rib is continuous (**Photo 3**).

Adjusting stitch numbers

When you have altered the number of stitches at casting on to get an even number remember to increase or decrease less or more stitches than the pattern indicates when you have to increase or decrease in the last row of the band. Thus, if the pattern tells you to increase 10 stitches in the last row of the rib, increase by 9 if you added an extra stitch when casting on, or by 11 if you cast on one less.

Example: If your pattern instructions state: 'Cast on 83 stitches and work 1 X 1 rib', cast on 82 or 84 stitches. If it states: 'Cast on 100 stitches and work in 2 X 2 rib', cast on 102 or 98, and adjust increases or decreases in the last row of the band accordingly, until you have the prescribed number of stitches.

Pocket tops and bands

For pocket tops, front bands and neck bands in a cardigan, the knit 1, purl 1 rib should have an uneven number of stitches. For pocket tops, starting with knit 1 and ending with knit 1 makes them look balanced. Front bands usually have a purl stitch next to a stocking stitch body, but have knit 2 at the edge at the front; on the wrong side start with knit 1, purl 1, as this will give you a neat garter stitch edge to help 'hold in' the bands. The neck band is usually a continuation of the front bands, so the same applies as for the front bands. This is discussed in detail in Chapter 13.

Sagging bands

While on the subject of bands, I suggest that when using cotton yarn or heavy wool, you use knitting-in elastic in the waist and wrist bands, but not for the neck band or the front bands for cardigans. The elastic will keep the bands from sagging and the garment will keep on looking good.

2 Increasing and decreasing stitches

Increasing

I find there are two particularly neat and satisfactory ways of increasing stitches:

1. Pick up the loop between the last and next stitch (see Diagram 3) and knit or purl into the back of it.

2. Make a half hitch (see Diagram 4) between the last and next stitch.

I use the first method for increasing stitches at each end of a row for sleeves, or for making increases in backs and fronts, and the second method for increasing stitches in the last row of bands.

Diagram 3: Pick up loop between 2 stitches

Decreasing

There are two methods commonly used to decrease stitches.

1. Slip one stitch, knit one stitch and pass slipped stitch over knit stitch (called sl 1, k1, psso). This method is used at the beginning of the knit row as the loops lie to the left. It can also be used at the beginning of a purl row, but substitute purl for knit.

2. Knit or purl two stitches together; this method is used at the end of a row, as the loops lie to the right.

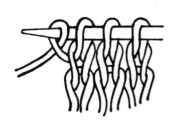

Diagram 4: A half-hitch

6

Increasing more than 2 stitches in a row

Increasing more than two stitches in one row occurs in almost every pattern in the last row of the bands, either at the waist or at the wrists. It must be done evenly, but once you have mastered the formula it is very easy.

Take the number of stitches to be added and divide it into the number of stitches already on the needle; this gives you the number of stitches after which you have to make a new stitch. As you cannot make a new stitch at the end of a row, and you often do not get an exact number when you divide, add the number of stitches after which you have to make a new stitch to the number you had left over after your division, and divide this number by 2. This will give you the number of stitches to work before the first new stitch and after the last new stitch.

Here are some examples, which will give you the formula to work out any number of increases.

Example 1: You have 60 stitches and want to increase to 67 stitches:
Step 1: 67 − 60 = 7 (7 new stitches will have to be made).
Step 2: 60 ÷ 7 = 8, with 4 stitches remaining (you make a new stitch after every 8 stitches).
Step 3: 8 + 4 = 12 (you add remaining stitches to step 2)
Step 4: 12 ÷ 2 = 6
So you will start with rib 6. Make a new stitch (by making a half-hitch or picking up the loop between the last and the next stitch, not by knitting twice in the next stitch, because that will throw your count into chaos), rib 8, etc. and end with rib 6, after the last new stitch.

Example 2: You have 82 stitches and want to increase to 90 stitches:
Step 1: 90 − 82 = 8 (8 new stitches will have to be made)

Step 2: 82 ÷ 8 = 10, with 2 stitches remaining; you make a new stitch after every 10 stitches
Step 3: 10 + 2 = 12
Step 4: 12 ÷ 2 = 6
The last row therefore reads: Rib 6, m1 (make 1 new stitch), rib 10, etc., end with rib 6, after the last new stitch.

Example 3: You have 36 stitches and want to increase to 48 stitches:
Step 1: 48 − 36 = 12 (12 new stitches will have to be made)
Step 2: 36 ÷ 12 = 3 (no stitches are remaining in this case, so you skip step 3)
Step 3: —
Step 4: 3 ÷ 2 = 1 and 2
The last row therefore reads: Rib 1, m1, rib 3, etc., end with rib 2, after the last new stitch.

Decreasing several stitches in one row

For decreasing a number of stitches in one row you can use the same procedure, but you have to remember to include the two stitches worked together in the amount after which you have to decrease.

Example: You have 98 stitches and want to decrease to 80 stitches.
Step 1: 98 − 80 = 18 (18 stitches will have to be decreased)
Step 2: 98 ÷ 18 = 5 (8 stitches remain). You decrease after every 5 stitches, which include the 2 stitches worked together.
Step 3: 5 + 8 = 13 (which includes one decrease, so deduct two stitches, leaving 11)
Step 4: 11 ÷ 2 = 5 and 6
The row therefore reads: Rib 5, decrease (working two stitches together), *rib 3, decrease*, repeat between *s and end with rib 6 after the last decrease.

3 'Locking in' stitches

Sometimes it is necessary to start a new ball of yarn in the middle of a row. It is always better to start a new ball at the side of the work, if it is at all possible, but occasionally you will have to start in the middle; for example, when you have a great number of stitches on the needle and run out of yarn before realising you were near the end of a ball, when you knit in the round on a circular needle or when the yarn you use is very expensive and you want to use every centimetre of it, and, of course, when you start a different colour.

It is then very helpful to 'lock in' the first stitch to avoid making holes in the work which you will have to close up later on. When working with different colours in jacquard knitting, locking in will help you avoid having to change threads to your right hand all the time, as you can keep the main colour over your right index finger and the contrast colour over your left index finger (see jacquard knitting, page 28).

Locking-in a knit stitch

To lock in a knit stitch, stick the right-hand needle into the next stitch as if to knit, wrap the old or main colour in your right hand under the right-hand needle, put the new or contrast colour on your left index finger over the right-hand needle and slip the old or main colour back the way it came (see Diagram 5). Pull the

Diagram 5: Lock-in knit stitch

stitch through and the new or contrast stitch is made. The formula, which is easily remembered, is 'under with the old, over with the new, back with the old thread'.

Locking-in a purl stitch

To lock in a purl stitch, stick the right-hand needle into the next stitch as if to purl, wrap the old or main colour in your right hand under the right-hand needle, put the new or contrast colour on your left index finger over the right-hand needle and slip the old or main colour back the way it came (see Diagram 6). Pull the stitch through (make sure that the yarn on your left index finger is to the left of the right-hand

Diagram 6: Lock-in purl stitch

needle, otherwise you will come up with 2 stitches instead of 1) and the new or contrast stitch is made.

Starting a new ball in the middle of a row

When you have to start a new ball of yarn in the middle of a row, you lock in the next stitch and continue with the new yarn, leaving the old yarn hanging at the back. When you have done 4 or 5 rows, pull up the locked stitch to the same tension as the surrounding stitches (check at the right side of your work). Then make a reef knot with the end of the old yarn and the beginning of the new yarn at the back of the work. (A reef knot is made with the left end over the right end, then the right end over the left end as in Diagram 7.)

Diagram 7: Reef knot

When you sew up your work later, put one thread of the knot into a bodkin (a fat stumpy needle with a blunt point and a large eye) and sew the thread diagonally up through the back of 3 purl stitches and the other thread diagonally down in the opposite direction through the back of 3 purl stitches (see **Photo 4**). This keeps the knot flat; it will not come undone and is nearly invisible.

This method will save time not only in jacquard knitting, as I have mentioned, but also in picture knitting, as you do not need to sew up the hole left otherwise when you change colour. When you darn in the threads afterwards, simply pull up stitches to the right tension (check on the right side of your work), make a reef knot and darn the ends into the loops of colour changes two or three times. Darn colour A through colour B loops, leaving the cut-off end above colour A, and darn colour B through colour A loops, leaving the cut-off end above colour B (see **Photo 5**), to make it as invisible as possible. When you cut the thread, leave a 1 cm end so it will not slip to the right side of the work.

When you darn in ends of yarn in jacquard knitting, you also pull up stitches to the required tension, make a reef knot and work the ends away in the strands on the back. Or you can weave in strands as you knit, since jacquard knitting works with horizontal lines.

If you have a single thread on the back of your work and you cannot make a knot, darn in thread as above, but at least five times instead of two.

4 Building up shoulders

Building up the shoulders so that the back and the front are higher at the neck than at the armhole, without casting off the stitches, can be done by 'short rows'.

Back shoulders

If your pattern reads: 'shape shoulders: cast off 10 stitches at the beginning of the next 6 rows', it means that 3 lots of 10 stitches are cast off for each shoulder. Instead of casting off, however, you can do this:

Work the next row to the last 10 stitches, bring the thread forward, slip the next stitch off the left-hand needle onto the right-hand needle, bring the thread to the back and put the slipped stitch back on to the left-hand needle. This stitch now has a wrap (see Diagram 8). Turn the work.

Diagram 8: Wrapped stitch

Work to the last 10 stitches, leave the thread in the front in purl, slip the next stitch from the left to the right-hand needle, bring yarn to the back and slip the slipped-off stitch back onto the left-hand needle, turn the work, bring the thread to the back.

Do these two rows again in the same manner, except that this time you work to the last 20 stitches and wrap the stitch as above; do the same on the purl row. Then once more, this time working to the last 30 stitches, wrapping the stitches as before.

You end up having turned the work after working to the last 30 stitches on the back of work. Now work to the end of the row, working the stitches that have been wrapped, together with the wrap, by slipping the wrapped stitch from the left-hand needle to the right-hand needle; with the point of the left-hand needle pick up the wrap and the stitch and slip the stitch back from the right-hand needle onto the left-hand needle so that you can now work them together (this gets rid of the loop at the bottom of the stitch).

Turn the work and work to the end of the row, working the wrapped stitches together with the wrap, but work through the back of the stitch; thus, if it is a purl stitch purl them together through the back of the stitches (see **Photo 6**) to prevent a loop appearing on the right side of your work.

Now you can put the stitches for the left shoulder on one stitch-holder, the stitches for the back neck on a second stitch-holder and the stitches for the right shoulder on a third stitch-holder. If you are short of stitch-holders, you can use a thread of approximately the same ply, but in a different colour.

Front shoulders

The shoulders for the front are usually done separately, because the front neck is lower than the shoulders. You work them exactly the same as the back shoulders, first the left shoulder, then the right shoulder.

When both the back and front (or fronts if you are working on a cardigan) have been finished, you still have all the stitches, which can now be joined (see page 12).

Another way of preventing holes in short rows is this: Work to the last 10 stitches, turn, slip next stitch purlwise, work to last 10 stitches, turn, slip next stitch, continue. When you have done all the building up, work to the end of the rows; when you come to a slipped stitch work that stitch plus the loop holding it (the loop your stitch comes through) together. At the back of the work, you work through the back of both loops, as with the first method.

Start building up the shoulders two rows earlier than the pattern indicates, as you do two extra rows at the end of the procedure.

Sleeves and body all in one

Using short rows instead of casting off stitches to build up shoulders can also be used for jumpers or cardigans which have the sleeves knitted onto the body—batwing patterns, for example. When you have knitted the sleeves to a certain height the pattern will say: 'Cast off X stitches at the beginning of Y rows'; this is to taper the sleeves. Instead of casting off, however, work to the last number of stitches indicated you had to cast off, e.g. cast off 5 stitches at the beginning of the next 20 rows. Instead of casting off, work to last 5 stitches, wrap stitch as described above, turn work, work to last 5 stitches, wrap stitch, turn work, and so on until 20 rows have been finished. After shaping the sleeves and the shoulders, you will still have all the stitches left. Graft them together so that there will not be an unsightly seam on top of the arm. It will look as if the knitting is continuous with the back of the sleeves, and there will be no seam at all.

5 Joining shoulders

There are two neat ways of joining shoulders, for both of which you need to have the stitches on the needles as shown in Diagram 8.

Method one

I use this method for textured knitting or for knitting with a pattern in it where a plain row would spoil the pattern, for example, Aran, fisherman's rib, lace knitting.

Put the stitches for the back shoulder on one needle (the same size as you used to work the main body) and the stitches for the front shoulder on a second needle of the same size. Hold the work in your left hand with right sides

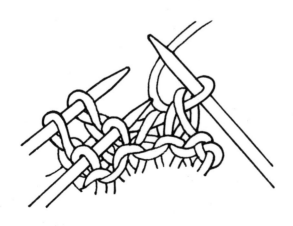

Diagram 9: Knit together stitches for shoulders

facing so the wrong sides are to the outside; with a third needle the same size as the other two knit the stitch from the front needle and the stitch from the back needle together (see Diagram 9) and slip off. Do the same with the second two stitches.

Now pull the first stitch over the second stitch, as you would when casting off. Continue like this until all the stitches have been used up. Pull the thread through the last stitch and work away end on the wrong side. If you do not have a third needle of the same size, use one of the needles you knitted the bands with to put the shoulder stitches on, not for knitting the join.

This method gives a nice smooth seam on the inside (see **Photo 7**) which when pressed is very inconspicuous on the right side of your work (see **Photo 8**). With this method the stitches of the back are exactly opposite the stitches of the front.

Method two

This method is used for all work done in stocking stitch, as you get an extra row of knit stitches between front and back. It can also be used for reverse stocking stitch and garter stitch.

Stocking stitch With the stitches of the back shoulder on stitch-holders, and one front shoulder finished with the stitches still on the needle, leave a long trail of yarn, approximately four times the length of the number of stitches to be cast off, and put it into a bodkin.

Put the stitches of the matching back on the second knitting needle. Hold both needles in your left hand, with the wrong sides of the work facing (so the right sides are to the outside), and your left index finger in between the two needles.

Insert the bodkin into the first back stitch from the back to the front (as if to purl), slip the stitch onto the bodkin and insert bodkin into the second stitch of the back from front to back (as if to knit); leave this second stitch on the knitting needle and pull the thread through. Now insert the bodkin into the front stitch from front to back (as if to knit), slip the stitch off the knitting needle onto the bodkin and insert bodkin into the second front stitch from back to front (as if to purl); leave this second stitch on the knitting needle and pull the thread through.

Continue like this until all stitches have been used up. Pull up the thread every time until made stitches fit snugly over your left index finger and are of the same tension as the knitted stitches. If they are too tight the row of stitches will look indented; if they are too loose it will look gappy. The best thing is to take it slowly and look carefully at each stitch made to ensure it is the same size as the rest of your knitting.

With this method the pattern is always half a stitch out and therefore not exactly opposite.

Reverse stocking stitch To join a pattern of reverse stocking stitch you can also use this method, but work the whole procedure in reverse.

Insert the bodkin into the first back stitch from front to back (as if to knit), slip the stitch onto the bodkin and insert bodkin into the second back stitch from back to front (as if to purl); leave this stitch on the knitting needle and pull the thread through.

Insert bodkin into the first front stitch from back to front (as if to purl), slip the stitch off the needle onto the bodkin and insert bodkin into the second front stitch from front to back (as if to knit); leave this stitch on the needle and pull the thread through.

Garter stitch If you are using this method for garter stitch, use the same method as for stocking stitch, as this makes 1 row of knit stitches between two rows of purl stitches and will make the rib continuous.

Different colours Where you have used different colours, for example in picture knitting, and the colour pattern on the back shoulders matches the stitches of the front shoulders, you can use method two equally well.

Leave a long tail of each colour. Thread the first colour onto the bodkin and work your way across the stitches until you come to the next colour. As the colours are half a stitch out, you work half the stitch into the next colour with the old colour, but instead of coming through the second stitch, you leave the thread on the inside, thread the bodkin onto the second colour and then come out to the outside through the second stitch, making sure the two threads are crossed on the inside of the work so there will be no hole. Thus, say, having worked all of the first colour at the front, stick the bodkin into the next stitch (the new colour) of the back, from the back to the front (as if to purl). Slip the stitch off the knitting needle onto the bodkin and pull the thread through the stitch.

Pull out the bodkin and thread the new colour onto it, cross the two threads on the inside and come out with the bodkin through the second stitch of the back, from the front to the back (as if to knit). Leave this stitch on the knitting needle and pull the thread through. Then carry on with the new colour as before, until you have to change colour again.

6 Sewing up work

In the first chapter I discussed casting on and how to make ribbed waist and wrist bands look continuous. When you carry on after the bands with whatever pattern you are using, the look of the seams will be improved if you keep the first and the last stitch in stocking stitch, that is, knit on the right side of the work and purl on the wrong side. This applies also to garter stitch.

When all the pieces of a garment are finished, blocked and pressed, you are ready to sew up. (You may have already joined the shoulders using the methods outlined in Chapter 5).

If you have made a jumper with set-in sleeves, sew up the side and sleeve seams before putting in the sleeves. If you have made a jumper or cardigan with the sleeves between two particular points joined flush to the front and back, sew the sleeves to the body first and then do the side and sleeve seams in one straight line.

Set-in sleeves

Let us start with the jumper with set-in sleeves. With the right sides showing, lay the back side seam next to the front seam (you can put a pin at the top, where the armhole starts, to hold them together). Thread the tail of the casting-on thread onto a bodkin. I usually leave a long

tail when casting on, and use it to sew up the side seam; it saves working away two threads at the bottom of the seam.

If you cast on as suggested in Chapter 1 and ribbed an even number of rows, the thread for the left seam will be on the back. Take the bodkin up into the cast-on stitch of the left front and pull the thread through. Bring the bodkin down between the first and second stitches of the first row of the back and up between the first and second stitches of the second row.

Then bring the bodkin down on the front between the first and second stitches of the first row and up between the first and second stitches of the second row.

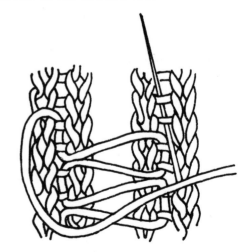

Diagram 10: Sewing up side seam

Then bring the bodkin down between the first and second stitches of the back (where you came up previously) and up two rows further on, always between the first and second stitches. Now bring it down between the first and second stitches of the front (where you previously came up) and up two rows further up (see Diagram 10).

I usually start off with 1 stitch only, or begin with 1 stitch only if I have to begin a new thread in the middle of the seam. Carry on in this way, always checking that you are working your way up evenly. If you find that the back is longer than the front, adjust by picking up only one loop between the first and second stitches of the front, while continuing with two of the back.

With this method you can see exactly what you are doing and make sure that patterns match precisely. The second row of the back lies nicely next to the second row of the front, so the seam is straight and nearly invisible. There is no sewing up from the wrong side with backstitch, where one frequently sticks in the middle of the next stitch and can create very wobbly, fat, hard seams.

You can see that this method is made much easier by keeping the first and last stitches in stocking stitch. Stocking stitch also has a way of curling over, which it does very nicely on the wrong side, so that the seam is very flat and smooth on the wrong side.

Sew up the sleeve seams in exactly the same manner as the front and back. If you have made the increases along the side seams as described in Chapter 2, it will be easy to stay one stitch away from the edge.

Now you are ready to set in the sleeve, again working with the pieces laid out right way up so you can see what you are doing. Measure the centre of the last cast-off row of the sleeve cap and pin that to the spot where the shoulder seam ought to be; I usually pin the sleeve halfway between side seam and shoulder seam as well.

If you have plenty of thread left from sewing up the sleeve seam or the side seam, use that for sewing the sleeve into the armhole, otherwise start a new thread.

Now pick up a stitch by the smaller end of the V, from either the sleeve or the body, depending on where your thread is, and as close to the edges as possible. When you come to the straight edge of the body armhole (where

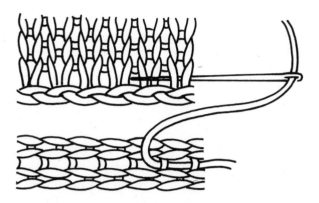

Diagram 11: Pick up loop or loops between first and second stitch of the body and the narrow end of the stitch just above the casting-off row of the sleeve

you stopped decreasing), pick up either 1 or 2 loops between the first and second stitches (as you did for side and sleeve seams), depending on how much the sleeve cap needs holding in; keep checking that the two sides remain equal. Work your way around the whole sleeve like this. At the place where the shoulder seam ought to be, adjust half a stitch closer to the edge of the body armhole. Work away the rest of the thread into one of the four seams.

To keep seams supple, while sewing up, pull them lengthwise now and then to ease tightness.

Dropped shoulders

For a jumper or cardigan with sleeves flush onto the body, first find the centre top of the sleeve and pin it to where the shoulder seam ought to be. Measure the depth of the armhole down from the shoulder seam on front and back and mark with a pin. Sew up the sleeves between the two pins, picking up 1 or 2 loops between the first and second stitches on the body, and 1 stitch from the sleeve by the short end of the V, as close to the edge as you can manage (see Diagram 11).

Keep checking that both sides work up evenly and adjust by picking up 1 or 2 loops, depending on how much the sleeve needs holding in. Fasten off thread in the seam. Starting from the bottom of the side seam work the bands. Continue up the side seam as for the set-in sleeve, up to the armhole and down along the sleeve seam. Finish off the wristbands the same way as waistbands. Work away the sewing thread and cast-on thread in sleeve seam on the wrong side.

Neckband

Now all that is left is to make the neckband. Starting from the left shoulder seam, pick up and knit the loop of the end stitch that is closest to you (see Diagram 12), not closest to the edge. It will be of considerable help if you have kept the first and the last stitches of your work in stocking stitch, as you can see the knit stitches lying at the edge and will know which loop to pick up.

Diagram 12: Pick up loop closest to you

When you come to the stitches which you have put on a stitch-holder for the front neck, count the stitches you have made so far and write down the number.

You can minimise holes between the picked-up stitches and the stitches you knit from the stitch-holders; by picking up the left loop of the stitch that is just beginning to lie to the right before the stitches on the stitch-holders, and the right loop of the stitch that comes just after the stitches on the stitch-holders and begins to lie to the left (see Diagram 13). Knit the stitches

Diagram 13: Pick up left leg of the stitch before the stitches on the stitch-holder, beginning to fall to the right. The right leg of the stitch after the stitches on the stitch-holder begin to fall to the left

from the stitch-holder, and then pick up and knit the stitches from the right side of the neck in the same way as the left side. Make sure you have exactly the same number of stitches on the right as on the left. When you come to the stitches on the stitch-holder for the back neck, knit them from the stitch-holder.

If you have the same number of stitches as your pattern says you should have, all is well. If, however, you have too many, cast off half the extra stitches in the side of the left neck as you start on the ribbing. (Make sure that you decrease by purling 2 together on the wrong side of the work and knitting 2 together when it is on the right side of the work; it will look neater.) Cast off the other half on the right neck.

If you have too few stitches, increase half the amount in the left neck by picking up a loop between two stitches and knitting or purling into the back of it; increase the other half in the right side.

Always knit the first row while picking up stitches so that all unevenness disappears to the wrong side.

Now finish the neckband in whatever way your pattern describes. If it is a 2 X 2 rib (knit 2, purl 2), cast off in rib. If, however, it is done in a 1 X 1 rib (knit 1, purl 1), it will look really nice if you finish with invisible casting off (see Chapter 7).

Photo 1: Invisible casting on in knit 1, purl 1 rib (page 4)

Photo 2: Cast-on straight edge (page 4)

Photo 3: Casting on in knit 2, purl 2 rib (page 5)

Photo 4: Ends worked away diagonally on the wrong side (page 9)

Photo 5: Work away threads with reef knot in 2 colours (page 9)

Photo 6: Purl through back of loops of wrapped stitch plus wrap (page 10)

Photo 7: Inside of shoulder seam (page 12)

Photo 8: Outside of shoulder seam (page 12)

Photo 9: Invisible casting off in knit 1, purl 1 rib (page 25)

Photo 10: Knitting in patches with the intarsia method (page 26)

Photo 12 below (page 29):
Top end: weave in thread on horizontal line of about 7 stitches. Sew other thread 4 or 5 times into loops of the second colour, so that thread end is above same colour. Bottom end: make reef knot and work each thread twice into loops of the second colour, so that thread end is above same colour.

Photo 11: Clear lines in rib (page 29)

Photo 13: Bobbles can give a special touch to an otherwise plain jumper. They can be knitted in the same colour as the jumper or in a contrasting colour (page 30)

Photo 14: First stitch of bobble backwards (page 30)

Photo 15: Finished buttonhole (page 31)

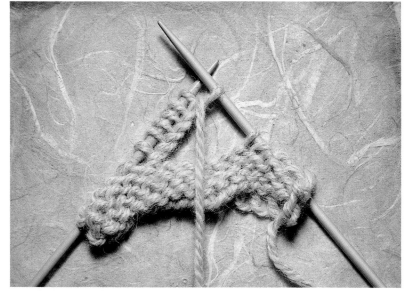

Photo 16: Yarn forward between last and last-but-one loop in buttonhole (page 31)

Photo 17: Embroidery stitch (page 37)

Photo 18: Cabling is used here to create diamonds (page 39)

Photo 19: Crewel or embroidery wool can be used for small amounts of colour. The colour range is extensive

Photo 20: Designing for intarsia work is easy; count the number of stitches and rows and work up the design on squared paper (page 40)

7 Invisible casting off

Invisible casting off on a knit 1, purl 1 row can be used for neck bands and pocket tops and on jumpers or cardigans that have been worked sideways, i.e. from one sleeve to the other, where you have to pick up the stitches from the body to make the waistband. In this case you end up having to cast off in rib; this also happens when sleeves have been worked from the top and you do the wristbands last.

Invisible casting off takes longer than normal casting off, but it is really worthwhile (see **Photo 9**), as you end up without that odd row of stitches lying down on top of the rib. Do not be put off thinking the method looks too complicated, because it is just like bicycling; once you have mastered it, you never forget it.

Step 1 Two rows before the desired length of the rib is reached, work as follows: Knit 1 (or 2 for cardigan neck bands and pocket tops), *wool forward, slip 1 stitch purlwise, wool back, knit 1*. Repeat between * and * to the last stitch, purl 1 or knit 1 on cardigan neck bands and pocket tops. In fact, knit the knit stitches, but slip the purl stitches purlwise with the yarn in front of the work. This helps prevent the rib from stretching. Leave a long, long tail (about four times the length of the stitches to be cast off), and thread it into a bodkin.

Step 2 Insert bodkin as if to knit into the second (purl) stitch and pull your thread through, then into the first (knit) stitch as if to purl, pull thread through and slip off the knitting needle. Now *insert bodkin into the second (knit) stitch as if to purl and pull thread through. Insert bodkin into the first (purl) stitch as if to purl, slip the stitch off the knitting needle (but leave it on the bodkin), go straight into the second stitch at the back of the work (as if to knit) and pull thread through. Next, insert bodkin into the first knit stitch from the front as if to knit, pull the thread through and slip the stitch off*.

At this stage give your thread a good tug down towards the back. Repeat between * and * to the last purl stitch.

If you work the neckband in the round with a circular needle, or 4 double-pointed needles, you can at this point insert the bodkin into the first cast-off stitch as if to purl, then into the last purl stitch as if to purl. Slip the stitch off the knitting needle and onto the bodkin. Insert the bodkin back into the first cast-off stitch and pull the thread through; you can then work away the tail in the back of the ribbing.

Once you have completed the casting off, slip the bodkin through the last stitch and use it for sewing up seams or pocket linings.

Where a neckband should be folded in half and slipstitched in place on the wrong side, it is better not to cast off the stitches, but to sew them straight off the needle to the first row of the neckband. This gives a nice supple neckband.

8 Knitting with two or more colours

Knitting patches (intarsia)

When knitting in patches (intarsia work) you work with one ball of yarn to where the patch starts, then lock in the next stitch with the second colour (as described in Chapter 3). When you have completed the stitches for the first row of the patch, lock in the next stitch with a new ball in the first colour and continue the row, either to the end or to the next patch. Thus for one patch you have three balls of yarn attached to your work, two in the main colour and one in the contrast colour.

On the next and subsequent rows twist the threads on the wrong side when you change

Diagram 14: Twist threads at the back for new colour

colour to prevent holes appearing in your work. To do this, work to the patch, lay the thread you were working with forward at the back of your work on a knit row or at the front of the work on purl row and pull the new colour from underneath (see Diagram 14). Continue with the new colour until you have to change colour again. Lay the colour you just worked with forward at the back of the work on a knit row, or at the front of the work on a purl row, pull the new colour from underneath and continue to work with that.

Tightening stitches   Remember when changing colour that the stitches on the left-hand needle may work themselves loose while you are using the different thread; therefore, before you stick your needle into the first stitch of that colour, pull down the thread of that stitch at the back. (Pull down, not up, because when you pull up, you only lift the loop of the stitch below and do not tighten the stitch.) You will see that not only will the first stitch on the left-hand needle tighten up, but the second stitch will also.

Colours out of step   Very often the stitches of the patch or patches are not directly above those of the last row and you have to start earlier or later on your contrast colour. Where there are 1 or 2 stitches difference, just twist the threads as above and make the next stitch as required.

However, very often you start the patch or patches 3 or 4 or even more stitches earlier or later than in the previous row. If you have to start, for example, 3 stitches earlier, lock in the new colour and continue on with it. If you start 4 or more stitches earlier, lock in the next stitch with the new colour and adjust the long loop you will get at the back. If the loop is too tight your work will pucker; if too loose, the stitch it came from will be bigger than the rest. You do, however, need a little bit of slack in order to knit under the loop, which will pull it up a little tighter.

Knit or purl one stitch with the new colour, but on the third, fifth, seventh, etc. stitch knit or purl with the new colour under the long loop you obtained after locking in the new colour. You do this in the first place to prevent long loops remaining at the back of your work, and in the second place to tighten up the stitches.

If you have to start 3 or more stitches later on the new colour, give a tug to the thread of your left finger at the back to tighten any slackness and work one stitch in the new colour. Work the next with the new colour under the old thread (which you keep over your left index finger), work the next over the thread on your left finger (see Diagram 15) and so on until you have done the required amount of stitches in the new colour. Then continue with the colour which was on your left finger. In this way you weave the old colour in with the new so that it will be there for you when you need it, and you prevent long loose loops at the back of your work.

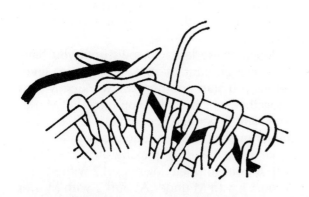

Diagram 15: Work under and over thread

Tangled yarn   Some people wind the yarns for different colours onto pieces of cardboard, or make separate little balls of yarn. I find that it is less time-consuming to use normal balls of wool, taking one thread from the outside and a second from the inside. This might tangle up at the back of your work as the two threads twist around each other as they unwind. If this happens simply pull the ball which seems to be the culprit so that the threads pull out of the tangle, then insert your finger between the two threads at the top and pull them apart while lifting up the ball. The ball will turn, untwisting the threads, or you can turn the ball yourself until the threads untwist.

To avoid twisting the threads at the back too much, make sure that you turn your work first one way then the other, not on and on in the same direction. If your threads twist so much that you cannot pull them through any more, take a ball with only one thread and work that through the tangle until it is clear, when the whole tangle will probably fall apart. If it doesn't, untangle one more ball and it will certainly do it then.

Small designs   If you have small design patches, you can use separate lengths of yarn, which you can measure off beforehand by counting stitches. For example, with an 8-ply wool count approximately 1 cm per stitch plus 12 cm at each end to sew in later. Small lengths of yarn are easily pulled through any tangles that may occur. I work daily with many different colours at the same time, and I can assure you that the tangles always look worse than they really are, and I very seldom have to lose time pulling balls of yarn through.

Using yarn other than 8-ply   If you want to work with individual lengths in yarns other than 8-ply, for example 5 or 12-ply, knit 10 stitches, hold the thread from where you left off in your left hand and pull out the 10 stitches, measure the amount and divide by 10 to give you the measurement for one stitch. Count the stitches you have to do, multiply with the measurement of one stitch, add 24 cm (allowing for 12 cm at each end to work away later) and you can cut your length of thread.

With mohair or brushed wool, or any hairy wool for that matter, the threads will tangle more and, because they rub together, form little rings of hair. To untangle, simply cut through this little ring with sharp-pointed scissors and the threads will be separated.

Jacquard knitting

In jacquard knitting you weave the second colour in at the back of the work instead of stranding the colour not in use. You work with two or three colours at the same time, one colour over your right index finger and the second colour over your left index finger, knitting under and over the colour not in use, as in picture knitting.

Here it is not a matter of a few stitches, but whole rows of knitting, very often in the round on a circular needle. You work the thread on your right index finger in the normal way. To use the colour on your left index finger you stick the knitting needle into the next stitch and with the point of the needle go over the thread on your left finger and pull it through the stitch. If you have to do more than 2 stitches with the colour on your left finger, on the third stitch lock in the colour on your right finger to bring it with you thus: Stick the knitting needle into the next stitch, go under with the colour on the right finger, over with the colour on your left finger, and back with the colour on the right finger the way it came (see Diagram 16).

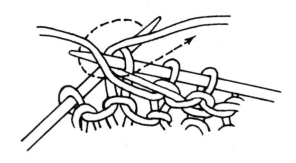

Diagram 16: Lock in stitch to bring thread with you

Sometimes you will find on the next row that some of the stitches which you picked off your left finger are twisted; simply knit or purl into the back of them and they will straighten out.

Using this method you can do Fair Isle knitting without making long loose loops at the back of your work. The only disadvantage of jacquard knitting is that sometimes stitches are not quite equal in size. This can be almost overcome by pulling those stitches that have the thread being taken along at the back trapped in with them, a bit tighter.

Some people knit or purl under and over on alternate stitches. I find, however, if you have 5 or more stitches, that knitting or purling 2 over the thread, then 1 under, then 2 over, makes the work a little less bulky.

Using a second colour intermittently

Sometimes a pattern calls for a second colour only every now and then. When the number of rows between the second colour rows is an even number, you can leave the thread of contrast colour attached, so that you do not have so many threads to work away afterwards. You can also take the second colour with you on the side of your work when you are knitting a striped pattern.

If your pattern reads, for example: 'With M (main colour) knit 3, *with A (contrast colour) knit 1, with M knit 7, repeat from*', you work as follows: With M on your right index finger and A over your left index finger, knit 3 with M, pick off the next stitch from your left index finger (being A), then knit 2 stitches with M over A, 1 stitch with M under A, 2 stitches with M over A, 1 stitch with M under A, 1 stitch with M over A, pick off next stitch from left finger to make one stitch with A, and so on.

In the next row work with M only. Next row work to last stitch with M, then work the last stitch with M under A to bring the thread of A with you.

Repeat these last two rows until you have done the amount of rows with M required, before you start another row working M and A together, which will be a purl row. Put M over your right finger and A over your left and purl the amount of stitches required with M, then make a stitch with A, picking off a purl stitch with A from your left finger, purl 2 with M over A, purl 1 with M under A, purl 2 with M over A, purl 1 with M under A, purl 1 with M over A, purl 1 with A, and so on.

Working different colours in rib

Sometimes a pattern calls for changes of colours in the waist and/or wrist bands, or even in front bands for cardigans. To keep clear, distinct lines in a striped pattern in the rib (see **Photo 11**), work the first row of the stripe all in knit (or purl, if it is at the back of the work), and continue the rib on the second row. Make sure to have knit over knit and purl over purl. This will not detract much from the elasticity of the bands. If you knit and purl on the first row, the purl stitches will show a loop of the old colour at the bottom of the stitch.

If you need to work patches in the bands, you can work them in the new colour in rib except on the first row. If you have to work two stitches, for example, in a new colour, do these stitches, *on the first row only*, in knit on the front of the work or purl on the back of the work.

On subsequent rows continue in rib on these stitches.

Weaving in threads at the back

To work away threads at the back is a rather tedious job. Sometimes you can eliminate the task by weaving in a thread that needs to be cut off at the end of a patch. Weave it under and over the new colour (on alternate stitches), but *on horizontal lines only*, and only where there are 8 or more stitches of the old colour (see **Photo 12**). If there are fewer than 8 stitches of the old colour, the thread is better worked away later with a bodkin or crochet hook, following the curve of the patch. Weaving threads into patches of a different colour will show through, so avoid doing it.

9 Bobbles

Bobbles (or popcorns, as the Americans call them) come in all shapes and sizes. Wherever they are required the pattern will give a description of the particular bobble needed for that garment.

Most bobbles are made by making several stitches into the next stitch, turning the work and then purling those stitches; the work is turned again and the stitches knitted again. The stitches are then pulled over the first stitch, or are worked together to reduce them again to 1 stitch.

Turning the work to do the stitches from the back is time-consuming and tedious, especially if you have to do several in one row. It is not really necessary—you simply work the stitches of the bobble backwards, from left to right. This applies *only* when the stitches are purled at the back of the work (see Diagram 17).

The first step in making bobble stitches puts them on the right-hand needle; you now insert the left-hand needle into the first stitch on the right-hand needle at the back of the work, from the front to the back; put your thread (which is on your right finger in the usual position) over the left-hand needle from the back to the front

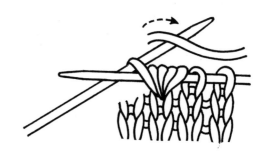

Diagram 17: Knit backwards for bobble. Insert left-hand needle into first stitch of the number of stitches you made for the bobble from front to back. Slip thread over left-hand needle from back to front and lift stitch over. Continue to do all bobble stitches the same way

(see **Photo 14**). This stops the stitch becoming twisted, which can cause problems later on the front when working them together. Pull the thread through and slip onto the left-hand needle. Do this until all the stitches of the bobble have been used up, then continue working the bobble stitches from the front in the way prescribed.

10 Buttonholes

To make neat buttonholes without loopy threads in the corners, one-row buttonholes are really marvellous (see **Photo 15**). They are made like this:

1. Knit to the first buttonhole. With yarn in front of work, slip first stitch from left-hand to right-hand needle, then place yarn at back of work and leave it there.

2. Slip next stitch from left-hand to right-hand needle and pass the first stitch over it; cast off one stitch. Continue to cast off stitches in this way until the stated number of stitches has been cast off.

3. Slip the last worked stitch back to the left-hand needle and turn work.

4. Place yarn to back of work (behind needles). Then cast on the same number of stitches as you cast off for the buttonhole, plus one extra stitch, as follows: *insert right-hand needle between the first and second stitches on the left-hand needle, draw through a loop and place loop onto left-hand needle for the first cast-on stitch; repeat from * until all stitches are cast on. Before slipping the last loop on the left-hand needle, bring yarn to the front to form a dividing strand (see **Photo 16**); turn work.

5. Slip the first stitch from left-hand needle to right-hand needle, pass the extra cast-on stitch over it to close the buttonhole, and pull the thread tight. Continue across the row.

11 Fixing some mistakes

Redoing a stitch lower down your work

If you have knitted through half the thread in a stitch somewhere down your work and have got an ugly loop in the middle of your garment, don't despair. Work the stitches on the needle until you get to the stitch directly above the mistake, and let the loop slip off the left-hand needle. Pull the work gently sideways until the stitch drops down. When you have come to the level of your mistake, stick your needle in the stitch under it. If you prefer use a crochet hook. If you use a knitting needle, put the lowest strand between knitted stitches over your needle together with the stitch and pull the stitch over the strand. Then take the next strand and so on until your stitch has reached the point where there are no strands left, and continue with your work (see Diagrams 18 and 19).

If the work is all in purl or in reverse stocking stitch, you can make purl stitches to fix the mistake, but it might be easier to turn the garment and work on the knit side.

Where the work is in seed stitch or garter stitch, you will have to make knit stitches and purl stitches alternately. To make a purl stitch have the strand of wool in front of the stitch on your needle and pull the strand through the stitch from the back.

Diagram 18: Picking up stitches with a crochet hook

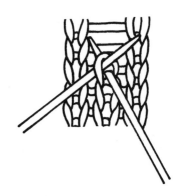

Diagram 19: Picking up stitches with knitting needles

Photo 21: Front bands can be
knitted onto fronts, which makes it
easy to carry colours through
(page 42)

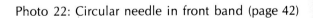

Photo 22: Circular needle in front band (page 42)

Photo 23: Two extra rows added to band to prevent puckering (page 43)

Photo 24: Two extra rows in front to hold in front band (page 43)

Photo 25: Front band stitches together with front neck stitches on stitch-holder (page 42)

Photo 26: Garter stitch edge on front bands (page 42)

Photo 27: Pockets can disappear in the overall pattern of the garment (page 44)

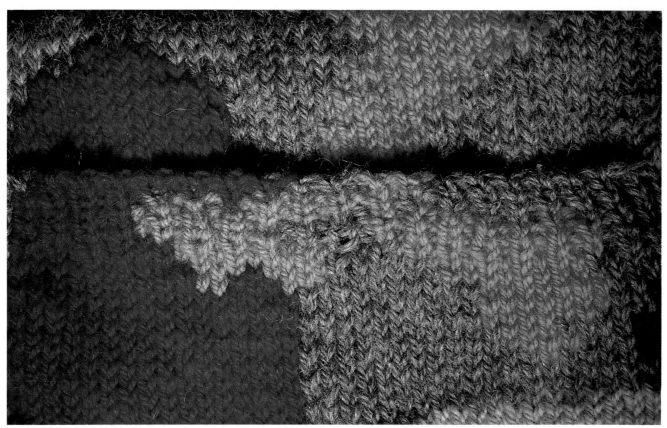

Photo 28: Pocket top knitted to blend in with rest of pattern (page 44)

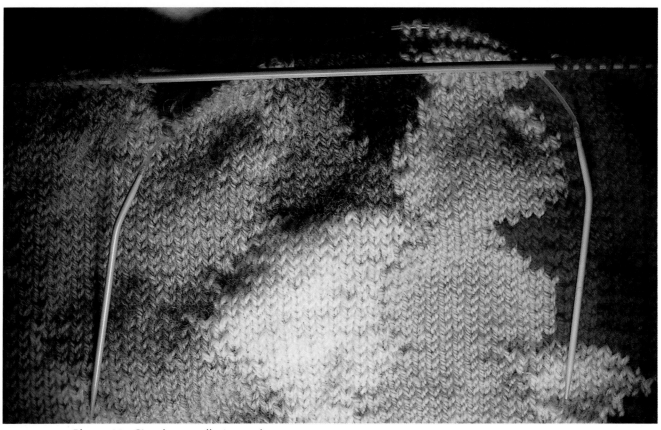

Photo 29: Circular needle in pocket top (page 44)

Adding colour in picture knitting

It's easy enough when doing picture knitting to start a colour a few stitches later than you should have. To save pulling out a row or two, start the new colour, leaving a long strand which you can use later to make the stitches with a bodkin in knitting stitch embroidery (see **Photo 17**).

Other small mistakes in picture knitting can also be put right with knitting stitch embroidery, working the right colour over the wrong one.

Loose stitches

A very loose stitch in the middle of the work can be adjusted by pulling up the stitch next to it, then the next, then the next, until you come to the edge. The edge stitch falls away to the back of the work when sewing up, so nobody will notice it.

Cables

Cabled the wrong way? Work across the row to the spot above the wrong cable, drop the 8 or 6 stitches to the place where you went wrong. Put half the stitches (4 or 3) on your needle and the other 4 or 3 stitches on the cable needle, and draw them over the first strand, first the ones on your needle, then those on the cable needle. Carry on until all strands have been used up. If you encounter more cabling on your way, just do this again.

Unravelling

If you have to unravel your work off the knitting needle, pick the stitches up again through the back of the loops with the right-hand needle and through the front of the loops with the left-hand needle.

With difficult yarn it might be better to unravel to one row above the mistake, put the stitches back on the needle and stick back the last row stitch by stitch, by sticking the point of the left-hand needle into the stitch below the first stitch on the right-hand needle. Slip off and the lower stitch will be on the left-hand needle (see Diagram 20).

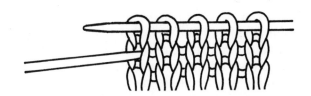

Diagram 20: Insert left-hand needle into stitch below the first stitch on the right-hand needle. Slip stitch off right-hand needle while pulling thread.

Starting a new thread of a different dyelot

If you are ever in the unfortunate position of running out of yarn for a garment and being unable to get the same dyelot, take some of the old yarn with you to the shop to get as close a match as possible.

To avoid a definite line between the old dyelot and the new one, you can do the following: keep some of the old yarn (enough to do three rows plus a bit extra) before starting on the new ball and leave it hanging at the beginning of your next row. Join the new yarn and work two rows with it, then leave it hanging and do two rows with the old yarn. Break off. Now do one row with the new yarn and break off. Do one row with the old yarn and break off. Rejoin the new yarn and continue to work the rest of your work with it.

Worked this way, a slight difference between the two dyelots will now be hardly noticeable—and probably not at all after the garment has been washed a couple of times.

Shortening or lengthening work

With right side facing, and working from left to right, slip a thin knitting needle into the right leg of stitches of the row just above the row you want to pull out. Cut through one leg of a stitch in the middle of the row immediately below the stitches on the knitting needle and pull threads out to the left and to the right until work separates.

Shortening To shorten, pull out as many rows from the bottom half as you need to plus one extra (this is to make up for the row of grafting stitches you will make) and put the stitches on a knitting needle of the same size as you used originally (the point must be facing the same way as the needle in the top piece). Make sure you have the same number of stitches on both needles.

Now graft the two halves together as described on page 12, ensuring that the tension is the same as before.

Lengthening To lengthen the work, put the stitches for the lower piece on a knitting needle, the same size as you used originally, and knit as many rows as necessary to obtain the length desired minus one row. Now graft the two pieces together as above.

Patterned work A patterned garment, for example one with cables, can still be shortened or lengthened, but it will have to be done in the 6 or 8 rows or so between cabling. In other patterned garments or multi-coloured patterns make sure you make or take away the right number of repeats to maintain continuity of the pattern.

12 Some hints on designing

The first question you will have to decide, if you wish to design your own garment, is what yarn you are going to use, and what needles. Whether you have in mind a cardigan, a jumper with long sleeves or a jumper with short sleeves, look up in pattern books for that particular yarn the approximate quantities you are likely to need.

Tension square

Make a tension square, using the needles you are going to use on the main body of the garment. Cast on about 25 stitches, in stocking stitch if you are going to do some picture knitting, or in the stitch you intend to use for your pattern. Do about 30 rows, which will give you sufficient space to measure how many stitches there are in 10 cm. If you are doing a picture from a graph, it is also necessary to count the number of rows per 10 cm; pure cotton, for example, will give you less rows per 10 cm than a man-made yarn. It is also important to know the number of rows per 10 cm to calculate how fast to increase for your sleeves.

Measurements

When you have worked out the number of stitches and rows per 10 cm, you then take the bust measurement, and add 5 cm or more for overwidth on front and back; measure also the length of your garment and sleeve length. If you want your garment to be 50 cm wide, for example, you then divide 50 by 10, multiply with the number of stitches per 10 cm, e.g. 22, which gives you 110. You will need 110 stitches plus 2 stitches for the selvedges for the body of your garment.

Cables

If you intend to include cables in your pattern, add 3 stitches for every 6-stitch cable, or 4 stitches for every 8-stitch cable. In fact, add 1 stitch for every stitch that is worked over another.

Bands

For the bands you use needles 2 or 3 sizes smaller. Cast on (for an 8-ply yarn) 8 to 10 stitches less than the body calculation. Take off more stitches if the body is to be very wide. Remember to have an even number of stitches for 1 X 1 rib and a number *not* divisible by 4 for a 2 X 2 rib.

Sleeves

For set-in sleeves you decrease about 5 to 6 cm, approximately 11 or 12 stitches for an 8-ply yarn; 6 or 7 stitches in the first two rows, then 1 stitch at each end 5 times to make the armhole sloping.

Shoulders

Shoulders can be shaped or straight. The front neck opening is started usually 5 to 8 cm lower than the back for an average size adult jumper, depending on whether you want a tight-fitting neck edge or a lower scooped-out one. For jumpers with set-in sleeves you calculate approximately one-third of the stitches for the left shoulder, one-third for the neck and one-third for the right shoulder. For the front neck put approximately half the stitches of the back neck opening on a stitch-holder and divide the rest of the stitches in half. Cast off half of that once and the remaining stitches on every other row to make the rounding for the neck edge.

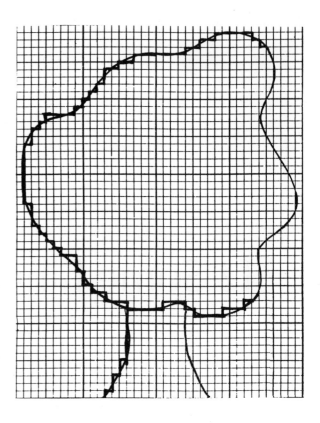

Diagram 21: Drawing on squared paper

Picture knitting (intarsia)

If you are going to knit a picture into your garment, make a graph on squared paper with exactly the same number of squares as you have stitches for the main body and the same number of squares for the number of rows above the bands. Draw the picture freehand on the paper, then work out the line you have to follow around the squares (see Diagram 21).

Remember to elongate pictures lengthwise, as there are more rows to the centimetre than stitches. You can buy knitting graph paper, which makes life easier.

Sleeves

Use the band from the back to measure around your wrist. This will give you the number of stitches needed for the sleeve band. In the last row of the band you can add a few stitches, depending on whether you like a bloused sleeve or a smooth-shaped one, say 0 to 6 in 8-ply for a smooth shape, and up to 20 or so for a bloused sleeve. Calculate the width of the

top of the sleeve by measuring the armhole length, double this for front and back, and work out the number of stitches you need; add 2 for selvedges. Deduct from that the number of stitches you have on the needle after increasing in the last row of the band, then see how many rows you need between the band and the top of the sleeve at the armhole. If, for example, you have to add 30 stitches, you have to make 15 increases of 1 stitch at each end; thus you divide the number of rows in the sleeve by 15 to give you the number of rows between increases.

If you like to start with the simpler straight sleeves, calculate how deep the armhole needs to be, and deduct that from the total length of the body of the garment. This will give you the length to armhole. When you have knitted up to that level knot a coloured thread at each end of the row, which will give you the points between which to calculate the width of the top of the sleeve. When you have finished, sew the sleeves in between the coloured threads.

To calculate sleeve length for a straight sleeve,

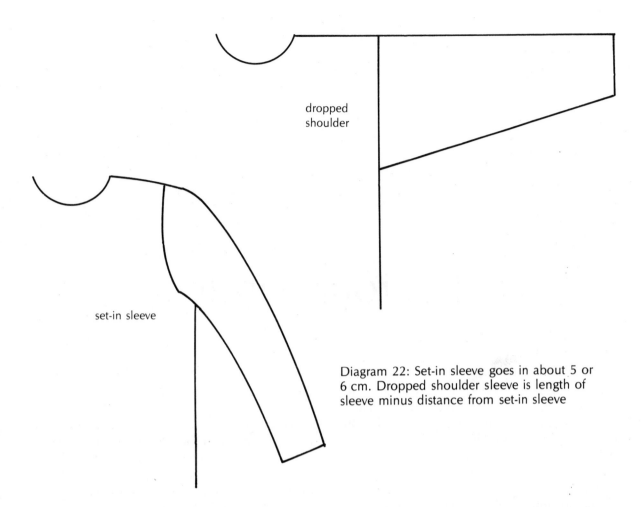

dropped
shoulder

set-in sleeve

Diagram 22: Set-in sleeve goes in about 5 or 6 cm. Dropped shoulder sleeve is length of sleeve minus distance from set-in sleeve

measure your normal sleeve length to armhole and deduct 5 or 6 cm, which you would normally have gone in for a set-in sleeve for armhole (see Diagram 22). This is because you will get a dropped shoulder. You then cast off all stitches in one row. If you would like a bit of a cap, you can cast off in about 7 rows.

Example If you have 114 stitches for the top of the sleeve (the top of the sleeve has approximately the same number of stitches as the back of the body), divide by 7, which is 16 with 2 stitches left over. Cast off 16 stitches at the beginning of the next 6 rows and (16 plus 2 =) 18 stitches on the last row.

13 Front bands

Although the front bands for a cardigan are generally knitted separately, they can be knitted on when knitting the fronts. This applies to cardigans with both straight fronts and V-necks, but *not* to front bands for which the stitches are picked up along the fronts and then knitted on outwards.

The advantages of knitting the bands on at the same time are that it is less laborious than doing them afterwards, you do not have to keep measuring them to see how long they should be, it is easier to make them both the same size, and you do not have to sew them on to the fronts, which is not as neat as knitting them on.

When a pattern advises you to put the stitches for the front bands (which were part of the waistband when casting on), onto a stitch-holder or safety pin to be finished off after the fronts are finished, keep these stitches and work them on the same size needles you used for the waistband while continuing the fronts with the larger needles. As it is a bit awkward to keep on using long needles for the front band here, it makes things a lot easier to use the shortest possible circular needle in the appropriate size (see **Photo 22**).

The main reason for doing the bands separately is that they can be made a little shorter than the fronts, and thus will hold their shape better, especially when heavy buttons are added. This is achieved by working short rows while the bands are being knitted on.

Buttonhole positions

Always start with the left front first for a woman's garment and with the right front for a man's. Mark the positions of the buttons with pins or coloured threads, which will make the positions for the buttonholes easy to work out.

Number of stitches

When you are making your bands with a knit 1, purl 1 rib, a better finish is achieved by working with an uneven number of stitches. Have the last 2 stitches of the left front band knit 2 on the right side, and start with knit 1 on the wrong side. Start the right front with knit 2 on the right side and end with knit 1 on the wrong side. This will give the outside edge of the front bands a neat garter stitch finish. (See **Photo 26**.)

The left front plus band should have an even number of stitches, since you start with knit 1 and end with knit 2. The right front plus band should have an uneven number of stitches, since you start with knit 2 and end with purl 1.

If you had to add or subtract 1 stitch from the number of stitches prescribed by the pattern to obtain an odd number, remember to adjust this when you start the main part of the fronts. If you have to increase in the last row of the band, increase 1 stitch less or 1 more. Also do not increase for the body in the stitches of the front bands.

Keeping bands in shape

To hold in the bands you work a few short rows. Hold up your work and, if it looks as if the band is beginning to sag a bit, work as follows: On the left front, work front to the last stitch before the band, wrap the last stitch as described on page 10, turn work and work wrong side to the end. On the next row work to the wrapped stitch, knit stitch and wrap together, and continue to work front band as before. The band now has two rows less than the front.

On the right front you do the short row on the wrong side as follows: Work to last stitch before the band, wrap stitch, turn work, and work next row to end. On the next row work to wrapped stitch, purl stitch and wrap together *through back of loops*, and continue on band as before (see Diagram 23).

The number of times you need to do this will depend on the kind of yarn you are using—pure wool keeps its shape better than cotton or man-made fibres.

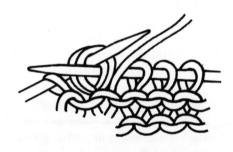

Diagram 23: Purl wrapped stitch plus wrap together on wrong side of work through back of loops

V-neck cardigan

The bands on V-neck cardigans also can be knitted on. Decrease stitches to form the V on the inside of the band by knitting two stitches together on the right side of the left front, and slip 1, purl 1, pass slipped stitch over, on the wrong side. Slip 1, knit 1, pass slipped stitch over on the right front on the right side and purl 2

together on the wrong side. Do not do any short rows in the V-neck shaping, as this should not be held in.

With a V-neck continue the front bands along the back neck until they meet at the centre back, where they can be grafted together.

Straight-front cardigan

With a straight-front cardigan, the stitches of the bands are kept on a pin when you reach the top of the centre front, together with the stitches you are supposed to cast off to shape the front neck, and are used afterwards to form part of the neckband (see **Photo 25**).

If the back neck stitches of a cardigan happen to be an even number, knit the two centre stitches together in the first row of the neck band to obtain an odd number for the entire neckband, since you work the neckband as the front bands with a knit 2 start and knit 2 end.

Colour changes

Colour changes in the front bands are also made easier by knitting them on. Do not start a colour change at the beginning or end of the band, but on the inside of the band. To keep lines straight, knit or purl the first row of colour change, continue in rib on the following rows.

Waist and wrist bands

Always have an even number of rows for waist and wrist bands, as the cast-on edge looks better when the first row is done on the right side.

Puckering in corners

To eliminate puckering in the corners when the front bands are knitted on, insert a couple of short rows in the bands at the first opportunity after the waist band has been completed, to make them longer there (see **Photo 23**). Rib the front band to the end, wrap the first stitch of the main body, turn work and rib back. On the next row rib to the end, work the first stitch of the main body and the wrap together and continue as normal.

14 Pockets

Pockets can be made without any interference to the pattern of your work, be it Aran or a multi-colour pattern. The only thing that will be different will be the pocket top. Even this, however, can be continued in the colours you are using for the body (see **Photo 28**), but will be made with knit 1, purl 1. (Where the bands have been done in knit 2, purl 2, you will have to do the pocket top in knit 2, purl 2 as well.)

Make the pocket linings as prescribed in your pattern and put the stitches on a stitch-holder. When you come to the point where the pattern says, 'Put X number of stitches [on which usually later the pocket top is knitted] on a stitch-holder', you work to the point where the pocket has to be inserted, and with the same size needles with which you did the bands, do the next X number of stitches in knit 1, purl 1. I use a small circular needle of the same size as the smaller needles (see **Photo 29**). Change to the bigger size needles and continue the row. Continue to work in this way with the pocket top stitches in the middle of your row on the smaller size needles, and in a knit 1, purl 1 pattern, until you have done the required number of rows for the pocket top (usually about 6 for an 8-ply wool).

On the next row (right side) cast off the stitches for the pocket top with invisible casting off (page 25). You will have to cut the thread, but leave a long tail, which you can use for sewing the pocket lining in place later. Attach a new thread and work to end of row. Next row: work to pocket top, insert the stitches from the stitch-holder for the pocket lining and work to end of row.

Different colours

When you use different colours in the ribbed pocket top, remember to work the first stitch of a new colour above the old colour in knit and not purl; you can purl the stitch again on the following row. Pocket tops with different colours look nicer if you knit the pocket linings with about 7 rows less than required; when it is time to insert them, work 7 rows in the colours according to your graph underneath the pocket top, ending with the last row of the pocket top. When the pocket opens a little, the lining won't show a difference in colour. The coloured threads are already there, so you can carry on with the threads in place.

The pocket top is now beautifully in place. Using this method the pocket tops do not have to be knitted on later and then stitched in place, which often results in uneven stitches and half stitches falling away because of the sewing.